# Vikingology
# Trivia
# Challenge

## Minnesota Vikings Football

# Vikingology Trivia Challenge

## Minnesota Vikings Football

## Researched by Paul F. Wilson

Paul F. Wilson & Tom P. Rippey III, Editors

## Kick The Ball, Ltd
Lewis Center, Ohio

# Trivia by Kick The Ball, Ltd

## COLLEGE FOOTBALL TRIVIA

| | | | |
|---|---|---|---|
| Alabama Crimson Tide | Georgia Bulldogs | Nebraska Cornhuskers | Oregon Ducks |
| Auburn Tigers | LSU Tigers | Notre Dame Fighting Irish | Penn State Nittany Lions |
| Boston College Eagles | Miami Hurricanes | Ohio State Buckeyes | Southern Cal Trojans |
| Florida Gators | Michigan Wolverines | Oklahoma Sooners | Texas Longhorns |

## PRO FOOTBALL TRIVIA

| | | | |
|---|---|---|---|
| Arizona Cardinals | Denver Broncos | Minnesota Vikings | San Francisco 49ers |
| Buffalo Bills | Green Bay Packers | New England Patriots | Washington Redskins |
| Chicago Bears | Indianapolis Colts | Oakland Raiders | |
| Cleveland Browns | Kansas City Chiefs | Pittsburgh Steelers | |

## PRO BASEBALL TRIVIA

| | | | |
|---|---|---|---|
| Boston Red Sox | Cincinnati Reds | New York Yankees | Saint Louis Cardinals |
| Chicago Cubs | Los Angeles Dodgers | Philadelphia Phillies | |

## COLLEGE BASKETBALL TRIVIA

| | | | |
|---|---|---|---|
| Duke Blue Devils | Indiana Hoosiers | Kentucky Wildcats | North Carolina Tar Heels |
| Georgetown Hoyas | Kansas Jayhawks | Michigan State Spartans | UCLA Bruins |

## PRO BASKETBALL TRIVIA

| | |
|---|---|
| Boston Celtics | Los Angeles Lakers |

Visit **www.TriviaGameBooks.com** for more details.

iv

*For Ann Wilson,*
*Jo & Jerry DeLoach,*
*Frank Wilson, Frankie & Cassiddee Partridge-Wilson,*
*Athena, David, Vivianna, Kaira, & Cheyenne Flierl,*
*Lani, Ray, Anthony, Marissa, & Sienna Puga,*
*David Wilson, Joanna Lawley, Ashton Wilson-Lawley,*
*& Isaiah Rodriguez*

Vikingology Trivia Challenge – Minnesota Vikings Football;
First Edition 2009

Published by
**Kick The Ball, Ltd**
8595 Columbus Pike, Suite 197
Lewis Center, OH 43035
www.TriviaGameBooks.com

Designed, Formatted, and Edited by: Paul F. Wilson & Tom P. Rippey III
Researched by: Paul F. Wilson

*For information on ordering this book in bulk at reduced prices, please email us at pfwilson@trivianthology.com.*

International Standard Book Number: 978-1-934372-66-1

Printed & Bound in the United States of America

10 9 8 7 6 5 4 3 2 1

# Table of Contents

## VIKINGOLOGY TRIVIA CHALLENGE

Dear Friend,

Thank you for purchasing our *Vikingology Trivia Challenge* game book!

We have made every attempt to verify the accuracy of the questions and answers contained in this book. However it is still possible that from time to time an error has been made by us or our researchers. In the event you find a question or answer that is questionable or inaccurate, we ask for your understanding and thank you for bringing it to our attention so we may improve future editions of this book. Please email us at tprippey@trivianthology.com with those observations and comments.

Have fun playing *Vikingology Trivia Challenge*!

*Paul & Tom*

Paul Wilson & Tom Rippey
Co-Founders, Kick The Ball, Ltd

PS – You can discover more about all of our current trivia game books by visiting www.TriviaGameBooks.com.

# How to Play

## Book Format:

There are four quarters, each made up of fifty questions. Each quarter's questions have assigned point values. Questions are designed to get progressively more difficult as you proceed through each quarter, as well as through the book itself. Most questions are in a four-option multiple-choice format so that you will at least have a 25% chance of getting a correct answer for some of the more challenging questions.

We've even added an *Overtime* section in the event of a tie, or just in case you want to keep playing a little longer.

## Game Options:

### One Player -

To play on your own, simply answer each of the questions in all the quarters, and in the overtime section, if you'd like. Use the *Player / Team Score Sheet* to record your answers and the quarter *Answer Keys* to check your answers. Calculate each quarter's points and the total for the game at the bottom of the *Player / Team Score Sheet* to determine your final score.

### Two or More Players –

To play with multiple players decide if you will all be competing with each other individually, or if you will form and play as teams. Each player / team will then have its own *Player / Team Score Sheet* to record its answer. You can use the quarter *Answer Keys* to check your answers and to calculate your final scores.

1

The *Player / Team Score Sheets* have been designed so that each team can answer all questions or you can divide the questions up in any combination you would prefer. For example, you may want to alternate questions if two players are playing or answer every third question for three players, etc. In any case, simply record your response to your questions in the corresponding quarter and question number on the *Player / Team Score Sheet*.

A winner will be determined by multiplying the total number of correct answers for each quarter by the point value per quarter, then adding together the final total for all quarters combined. Play the game again and again by alternating the questions that your team is assigned so that you will answer a different set of questions each time you play.

**You Create the Game** -
There are countless other ways of using **Vikingology Trivia Challenge** questions. It is limited only to your imagination. Examples might be using them at your tailgate or other pro football related party. Players / Teams who answer questions incorrectly may have to perform a required action, or winners may receive special prizes. Let us know what other games you come up with.

Have fun!

# First Quarter

*1-Point Questions*

1) Minnesota Vikings owners forfeit their AFL membership to join the NFL.

    A) True
    B) False

2) What are the Vikings' team colors?

    A) Yellow and Purple
    B) Yellow and White
    C) Purple, Yellow, and Black
    D) Purple, Gold, and White

3) What year did Metropolitan Stadium open?

    A) 1956
    B) 1961
    C) 1976
    D) 1985

4) What year did Minnesota play its first-ever game?

    A) 1941
    B) 1951
    C) 1961
    D) None of the above

5) What was Vikings head coach Harry Peter Grant Jr.'s nickname?

    A) Pete
    B) Bud
    C) H.P.
    D) Gus

6) In which NFL Division does Minnesota play?

    A) NFC North
    B) NFC South
    C) NFC East
    D) NFC West

7) What is the name of Minnesota's team song?

    A) "V-I-K-I-N-G-S!"
    B) "Skol, Vikings"
    C) "Minnesota Rouser"
    D) "Vikings, Salute"

8) How many times did the Vikings play the College All-Stars?

    A) 0
    B) 3
    C) 6
    D) 9

# *First Quarter*   *1-Point Questions*

9) Who did the Vikings draft with their one and only Bonus Choice pick?

    A) Fran Tarkenton
    B) Tommy Mason
    C) Steve Stonebreaker
    D) None of the above

10) How many miles does the average Metrodome vendor walk during a Vikings home game?

    A) 2
    B) 5
    C) 7
    D) 10

11) Who was the most recent Vikings head coach to win Associated Press (AP) NFL Coach of the Year?

    A) Brad Childress
    B) Dennis Green
    C) Mike Tice
    D) Bud Grant

12) The popular horned hats with braids worn by Vikings fans are called Helga hats.

    A) True
    B) False

**13)** What position did Vikings coach Brad Childress play in college?

    A) Quarterback
    B) Punter
    C) Cornerback
    D) None of the above

**14)** What is the name of the horn played at Vikings games?

    A) Nordic
    B) Fluegelhorn
    C) Gjallarhorn
    D) Alpenhorn

**15)** Did Fran Tarkenton start eight games for the Vikings his rookie season?

    A) Yes
    B) No

**16)** When was the most recent season Minnesota did not play a Monday Night Football (MNF) game?

    A) 1987
    B) 1994
    C) 2003
    D) 2008

# First Quarter
*1-Point Questions*

**17)** The Hubert H. Humphrey Metrodome owes which of its nicknames to its acoustic qualities?

    A) The Dome
    B) Thunderdome
    C) The Eggshell
    D) Homerdome

**18)** From which school have the Vikings drafted the most players?

    A) Notre Dame
    B) Southern Cal
    C) Wisconsin
    D) Minnesota

**19)** Who holds Minnesota's career rushing yards record?

    A) Chuck Foreman
    B) Robert Smith
    C) Adrian Peterson
    D) Bill Brown

**20)** How many weeks were Vikings players named NFL Rookie of the Week in 2008?

    A) 0
    B) 2
    C) 5
    D) 7

# First Quarter

21) The H.H.H. Metrodome has a seating capacity over 65,000.

    A) True
    B) False

22) What year did the Viking horn first appear on Minnesota's helmets?

    A) 1961
    B) 1968
    C) 1976
    D) 1982

23) Which Minnesota head coach has the most career wins?

    A) Dennis Green
    B) Jerry Burns
    C) Bud Grant
    D) Norm Van Brocklin

24) What year did Zygmunt "Zygi" Wilf purchase the Minnesota Vikings from Red McCombs?

    A) 2004
    B) 2005
    C) 2006
    D) 2007

# *First Quarter*

*1-Point Questions*

25) Who holds Minnesota's record for passing yards in a single game?

    A) Tommy Kramer
    B) Daunte Culpepper
    C) Warren Moon
    D) Randall Cunningham

26) What is the name of the proposed new stadium for Vikings football?

    A) Minnesota Stadium
    B) Twin Cities Center
    C) Minneapolis-St. Paul Field
    D) Vikings Stadium

27) How many times has Minnesota played in the Super Bowl?

    A) 2
    B) 4
    C) 5
    D) 6

28) Where do the Vikings hold their annual training camp?

    A) Duluth, Minn.
    B) Edina, Minn.
    C) Mankato, Minn.
    D) Moorhead, Minn.

# First Quarter

29) Have the Vikings ever played the Packers in the postseason?

    A) Yes
    B) No

30) How many times has a Viking had greater than 2,000 combined net yards in a single season?

    A) 2
    B) 3
    C) 5
    D) 6

31) Who led the Vikings in sacks during the 2008 regular season?

    A) Kevin Williams
    B) Jared Allen
    C) Chad Greenway
    D) Antoine Winfield

32) Which team has Minnesota played the most in postseason games?

    A) Washington Redskins
    B) San Francisco 49ers
    C) Dallas Cowboys
    D) St. Louis Rams

# *First Quarter*

33) What are the most regular-season wins the Vikings have had in a single season?

    A)  11
    B)  13
    C)  15
    D)  16

34) Which Viking holds the NFL record for most touchdowns in a rookie season?

    A)  Randy Moss
    B)  Buster Rhymes
    C)  Troy Williamson
    D)  Hassan Jones

35) How many defensive TDs did the Vikings have in 2008?

    A)  0
    B)  2
    C)  5
    D)  9

36) What single-season NFL record did the Vikings set in 1981?

    A)  Fewest Points After Touchdown (PAT)
    B)  Fewest Times Sacked
    C)  Most Yards Gained Rushing
    D)  Most Passes Attempted

# First Quarter
*1-Point Questions*

37) Who is the play-by-play announcer for the Vikings Radio Network?

    A) Paul Allen
    B) Greg Coleman
    C) Jeff Dubay
    D) Pete Bercich

38) Gus Frerotte had a better completion percentage in the Vikings' 2008 regular season than Tarvaris Jackson.

    A) True
    B) False

39) In the lyrics of Minnesota's fight song, what color is identified?

    A) Purple
    B) Gold
    C) White
    D) None of the above

40) What is the name of the Vikings' official drum line?

    A) Skol Line
    B) Skol Corps
    C) Bangers
    D) Helga Drummers

# *First Quarter*

41) How many NFL opponents have never beaten the Vikings at home?

    A)  0
    B)  1
    C)  2
    D)  3

42) Who holds Minnesota's record for receiving yards in the regular season?

    A)  Cris Carter
    B)  Randy Moss
    C)  Rickey Young
    D)  Ahmad Rashad

43) What year was the famous "Hail Mary" pass thrown by Dallas's Roger Staubach against Minnesota?

    A)  1975
    B)  1978
    C)  1982
    D)  1987

44) How many NFL Championships has Minnesota won?

    A)  1
    B)  2
    C)  4
    D)  5

# First Quarter

*1-Point Questions*

**45)** Which Viking holds the team's single-game rushing record?

    A) Michael Bennet
    B) Chuck Foreman
    C) Adrian Peterson
    D) Chester Taylor

**46)** How many Vikings have been named Super Bowl MVP?

    A) 1
    B) 2
    C) 4
    D) None of the above

**47)** How many one-season head coaches has Minnesota had?

    A) 1
    B) 2
    C) 3
    D) 4

**48)** Did Bud Grant coach another professional football team after leaving the Vikings?

    A) Yes
    B) No

49) Who holds Minnesota's record for points scored in a career?

    A) Cris Carter
    B) Fuad Reveiz
    C) Gary Anderson
    D) Fred Cox

50) What season did the Vikings celebrate their first-ever victory over Green Bay?

    A) 1961
    B) 1964
    C) 1970
    D) 1973

# First Quarter Viking Cool Fact

Since 1982 the Hubert H. Humphrey Metrodome has been the Vikings' twelfth man. The structure's self-supporting roof is an engineering marvel requiring 250,000 cubic feet of air pressure per minute to stay inflated. Approximately twenty 90-horsepower electric fans do the job of keeping the roof inflated – inflating the Vikings' spirits however, takes a fan of an entirely different color. Dare I say purple and gold? Although the Metrodome is one of the NFL's smallest venues at its 64,000+ seating capacity, it is easily one of its loudest. Opponents sometimes prepare for games in the Thunderdome by adding crowd noise to their practices. It might be impossible, though, to prepare for the jet-engine decibel levels (118-125dB) that are frequently recorded under the dome's ten acres of Teflon-coated fiberglass. In fact, OSHA suggests limiting exposure to this noise level to a quarter hour or less per day. When applied in key moments during a game, the Vikings' twelfth man's cheers thwart the opposition's communication, rhythm, and inevitably their chances of victory.

# *First Quarter Answer Key*

1) A – True (Founders E. William Boyer, Ole Haugsrud, Bernard H. Ridder, H.P. Skoglund, and Max Winter elected to join the NFL as an expansion team in lieu of the competing AFL.)

2) D – Purple, Gold, and White (Colors chosen perhaps because they are as bold as the Viking culture.)

3) A – 1956 (The Met officially opened on April 24, 1956. It was built for minor league baseball.)

4) C – 1961 (On Sept. 17, 1961, 32,236 fans watched the Vikings play their first-ever regular-season NFL game.)

5) B – Bud (Born Harry Peter Grant, Jr., his mother nicknamed him "Buddy Boy", which was later shortened to simply Bud.)

6) A – NFC North (Minnesota joined the NFC North as part of the NFL's 2002 division realignment.)

7) B – "Skol, Vikings" (Written by Red McCloud of Edina, Minn. for the Vikings circa 1961.)

8) A – 0 (The NFL Champion played the College All-Stars for 42 years from 1934-76. Despite having won an NFL Championship in 1969, it was the Super Bowl Champions who played the All-Stars that season.)

9) D – None of the above (Bonus Choice picks were held from 1947-58, prior to the Vikings entering the NFL.)

10) B – 5 (Much of this walking is up and down Metrodome stairs.)

11) D – Bud Grant (Coach Grant is the only Vikings head coach to ever win the prestigious award.)

12) A – True (Varieties of the hat include metal and crochet options.)

13) D – None of the above (A 1988 graduate of Eastern Illinois, Childress did not play college football.)

14) C – Gjallarhorn (The horn is played to signal the start of all home games.)

15) A – Yes (He started 8 of 14 games in 1961.)

16) C – 2003 (It was the first season since 1986 that the Vikings had not played in a MNF game.)

17) B – Thunderdome (Decibel levels up to 125 have been recorded in the dome. This is louder than many rock concerts, giving Minnesota a decided home-field advantage.)

18) D – Minnesota (All-time, the Vikings have drafted 19 players from UM. The most recent was defensive back Tyrone Carter [Round 4, Pick 24] in 2000.)

19) B – Robert Smith (With 6,818 career rushing yards, Smith leads all Vikings rushers.)

20) A – 0 (Adrian Peterson was the most recent Viking to receive the honor [twice in 2007].)

21) B – False (Official seating capacity for Vikings football is 64,121.)

22) A – 1961 (Since their entry into the league, Vikings helmets have always featured a Viking horn.)

23) C – Bud Grant (Coach Grant had 158 career wins as Minnesota's head coach from 1967-83 and 1985.)

24) B – 2005 (The real estate magnate from New Jersey and his group of investors purchased the team for $600 million.)

25) A – Tommy Kramer (490 yards at Washington Redskins on Nov. 2, 1986 [Minn. 38, Wash. 44 (OT)].)

26) D – Vikings Stadium (The Vikings proposed new home would include a retractable roof and has an estimated construction cost of nearly $1 billion.)

27) B – 4 (Super Bowls IV, VIII, IX, and XI)

28) C – Mankato, Minn. (The Vikings have held their training camp at Minnesota State University in Mankato for 44 consecutive seasons.)

29) A – Yes (Minnesota played its first-ever postseason game against Green Bay on Jan. 9, 2005 in the NFC Wild Card game [Minn. 31, Green Bay 17].)

30) A – 2 (Adrian Peterson 2,021 [1,341 rushing, 412, return, and 268 receiving] in 2007 and Herschel Walker 2,051 [770 rushing, 966 return, and 315 receiving] in 1990)

31) B – Jared Allen (DE Jared Allen had 14.5 team-leading sacks in the 2008 regular season.)

32) D – St. Louis Rams (Seven: six games as the L.A. Rams [1988, 1978, 1977, 1976, 1974, and 1969] and one game as St. Louis Rams [1999])

33) C – 15 (In 1998 the Vikings ended the season with a 15-1 regular-season record.)

34) A – Randy Moss (In his rookie season of 1998 Moss had an NFL-record setting 17 TDs.)

35) B – 2 (Antoine Winfield and Napoleon Harris each had one defensive TD in 2008.)

36) D – Most Passes Attempted (Minnesota's record setting 709 pass attempts led to 382 completions, 29 interceptions, and 6.4 yards per attempt.)

37) A – Paul Allen (Allen has been the Vikings Radio Network play-by-play announcer since 2002.)

38) B – False (Both passers had a 59.1% completion percentage in 2008. Frerotte completed 178 of 301 passes and Jackson 88 of 149.)

39) D – None of the above (No colors are included in the lyrics of "Skol, Vikings".)

40) A – Skol Line (The line performs at games, tailgates, and other team-related events.)

41) D – 3 (Cincinnati [4-0], Houston [1-0], and Baltimore [0-0]. The Ravens are scheduled to visit the Vikings for the first time in Week 6 of the 2009 season.)

42) B – Randy Moss (Set with 1,632 receiving yards in 2003)

43) A – 1975 (The last-second desperation pass allowed the Cowboys to defeat Minnesota in the 1975 NFC Divisional Playoff game [Minnesota 14, Dallas 17].)

44) A – 1 (Minnesota won the NFL Championship earning the right to meet the AFL's Kansas City Chiefs in Super Bowl IV.)

45) C – Adrian Peterson (Peterson set Minnesota's and the NFL's single-game rushing yards record with 296 yards on Nov. 4, 2007 vs. San Diego.)

46) D – None of the above (No Vikings won the award in any of the team's Super Bowl appearances.)

47) A – 1 (Les Steckel is the only coach to the lead the team for only one year.)

48) B – No (Coach Grant did not coach another team after his 1985 one-year return to coaching the Vikings.)

49) D – Fred Cox (Cox scored 1,365 career points from 1963-77 [519 PATs and 282 FGs].)

50) B – 1964 (After three seasons of failed attempts, Minnesota defeated Green Bay 24-23 on Oct. 4, 1964 at Lambeau Field.)

Note: All answers valid as of the end of the 2008 season, unless otherwise indicated in the question itself.

# Second Quarter
*2-Point Questions*

1) What is the name of the stadium on MSU, Mankato's campus where Vikings summer training camp is held?

   A) Blakeslee Stadium
   B) Mankato Outdoor Stadium
   C) Blackrock Field
   D) Reilly Field

2) What jersey number did the Vikings' Fran Tarkenton wear?

   A) #7
   B) #8
   C) #9
   D) #10

3) When was the last time the Vikings drafted a running back in the first round?

   A) 2001
   B) 2002
   C) 2007
   D) 2008

4) Which decade did Minnesota have the best winning percentage?

   A) 1970s
   B) 1980s
   C) 1990s
   D) 2000s

5) Does Minnesota have an all-time winning record against Chicago?

    A) Yes
    B) No

6) What is Minnesota's record for most consecutive 10-win seasons?

    A) 2
    B) 3
    C) 4
    D) 5

7) What are the most rushing yards by the Vikings in a Super Bowl?

    A) 67
    B) 71
    C) 72
    D) None of the above

8) Where did the Vikings' Bud Grant play college football?

    A) Minnesota
    B) Wisconsin
    C) Navy
    D) Illinois

9) For which college did the Vikings' Randy Moss, Doug Chapman, and Carl Lee play?

- A) Missouri
- B) Texas
- C) Florida
- D) Marshall

10) Do the Vikings have a winning record in games following a bye week?

- A) Yes
- B) No

11) What are the most points the Vikings allowed in a postseason game?

- A) 41
- B) 43
- C) 49
- D) 52

12) How many teams has Minnesota played 50 or more times in the regular season?

- A) 4
- B) 6
- C) 8
- D) 10

# Second Quarter *2-Point Questions*

13) Does Minnesota's Tarvaris Jackson have greater than 500 career passing attempts?

   A) Yes
   B) No

14) Who was the last player to gain greater than 200 yards rushing against Minnesota?

   A) Terrell Davis
   B) James Wilder
   C) LaDainian Tomlinson
   D) Barry Sanders

15) What is the Metrodome record for longest field goal kicked by a Viking?

   A) 50 yards
   B) 56 yards
   C) 59 yards
   D) 61 yards

16) Which of the following Vikings never led the league in scoring?

   A) Fred Cox
   B) Gary Anderson
   C) Cris Carter
   D) None of the above

# Second Quarter *2-Point Questions*

**17)** Against which team was Minnesota's first NFL win?

    A) San Francisco 49ers
    B) Chicago Bears
    C) Baltimore Colts
    D) Dallas Cowboys

**18)** When was the last time the Vikings had over 500 yards of total offense in a postseason game?

    A) 1976
    B) 1987
    C) 2000
    D) Has never happened

**19)** How many times has Minnesota had the number one overall draft pick?

    A) 0
    B) 1
    C) 2
    D) 3

**20)** His job at Minnesota is Brad Childress's first head coaching position at any level.

    A) True
    B) False

# Second Quarter  *2-Point Questions*

21) How many yards is the longest rushing play in Minnesota history?

    A)  80
    B)  85
    C)  90
    D)  95

22) Which team has Minnesota never beaten at home?

    A)  New York Jets
    B)  New England Patriots
    C)  Jacksonville Jaguars
    D)  None of the above

23) For which original founder is the Vikings' training facility named?

    A)  Ole Haugsrud
    B)  Max Winter
    C)  Bernard H. Ridder
    D)  H.P. Skoglund

24) How many times has Minnesota played in the NFC Wild Card Playoff Game?

    A)  5
    B)  7
    C)  9
    D)  11

# Second Quarter *2-Point Questions*

25) The Vikings were outgained in all of their Super Bowl appearances.

    A) True
    B) False

26) What year did the Vikings win their first-ever postseason game?

    A) 1962
    B) 1964
    C) 1966
    D) 1969

27) How many times has Minnesota lost a season opener played at home?

    A) 1
    B) 4
    C) 7
    D) 11

28) How many Minnesota players have been named AP NFL Offensive Rookie of the Year?

    A) 4
    B) 5
    C) 6
    D) 7

# Second Quarter   *2-Point Questions*

29) How many years did Mike Tice play football for the Vikings?

    A) 0
    B) 1
    C) 2
    D) 3

30) How many total preseason and regular-season games did Minnesota play in its first-ever NFL season?

    A) 18
    B) 19
    C) 20
    D) 21

31) What is Minnesota's all-time longest recorded punt?

    A) 75 yards
    B) 78 yards
    C) 81 yards
    D) 84 yards

32) Do the Vikings have an all-time winning record against the AFC?

    A) Yes
    B) No

# Second Quarter  *2-Point Questions*

33) Who was the most recent Viking to have over 100 receptions in a single season?

   A)  Randy Moss
   B)  Cris Carter
   C)  Bobby Wade
   D)  Bernard Berrian

34) Who is the only Viking to have greater than 250 receiving yards in a single game?

   A)  Paul Flatley
   B)  Sammy White
   C)  Randy Moss
   D)  None of the above

35) To which team did Minnesota suffer its worst loss in its first NFL season?

   A)  Green Bay Packers
   B)  Dallas Cowboys
   C)  Chicago Bears
   D)  Los Angeles Rams

36) Who was Minnesota's first opponent at the Metrodome?

   A)  Tampa Bay Buccaneers
   B)  Detroit Lions
   C)  Baltimore Colts
   D)  New York Jets

# Second Quarter

*2-Point Questions*

37) How many yards was the Vikings' longest touchdown drive in 2008?

    A) 80
    B) 82
    C) 95
    D) 99

38) Which Viking played in the most Pro Bowls?

    A) Alan Page
    B) Randall McDaniel
    C) Cris Carter
    D) Ron Yary

39) Who holds Minnesota's record for passing yards in a season?

    A) Joe Kapp
    B) Fran Tarkenton
    C) Daunte Culpepper
    D) Warren Moon

40) In 2007 the Vikings led the NFL in both rushing offense and rushing defense.

    A) True
    B) False

# *Second Quarter* *2-Point Questions*

41) Who holds Minnesota's record for receiving yards in a single regular-season game?

    A) Randy Moss
    B) Sammy White
    C) Paul Flatley
    D) Anthony Carter

42) How many starting QBs did Minnesota have during Fran Tarkenton's five seasons away from the team?

    A) 1
    B) 2
    C) 3
    D) 4

43) Who holds Minnesota's record for most consecutive punts with no blocks?

    A) Chris Kluwe
    B) Harry Newsome
    C) Mitch Berger
    D) Greg Coleman

44) How many Vikings have recorded over 1,000 career tackles?

    A) 2
    B) 3
    C) 6
    D) 7

45) Did Fran Tarkenton have greater than 30,000 career passing yards?

    A) Yes
    B) No

46) Who holds the Vikings' record for career sacks?

    A) Alan Page
    B) Jim Marshall
    C) John Randle
    D) Carl Eller

47) How many Vikings had over 1,250 yards receiving in a single season?

    A) 2
    B) 4
    C) 6
    D) 8

48) How many Minnesota head coaches have been named NFL Coach of the Year?

    A) 1
    B) 2
    C) 3
    D) 4

49) How many different decades have the Vikings won at least 85 games?

    A)  1
    B)  2
    C)  3
    D)  4

50) Who is the only Viking honored with the Walter Payton Award – NFL Man of The Year?

    A)  Cris Carter
    B)  Adrian Peterson
    C)  Alan Page
    D)  Randy Moss

# Second Quarter Viking Cool Fact

Opponents can sometimes be heard praying for a victory over the Vikings. On at least one occasion, an answer to that prayer was delivered. Is it a dubious distinction to be known as the team on the wrong end of a pass forever known as The Hail Mary? Or maybe, every time the term is uttered it should conjure images of arguably one of the NFL's greatest endings (and lessons from certain aspects of its aftermath). Generations of school-yard boys have yelled Hail Mary as recess bells fill the air. Most of them may not know the term originates from the classic 1975 game between the Vikings and the Cowboys. They should know how the Vikings took a 14-10 lead into the final moments of the game, how countless fans held their breath as Roger Staubach's pass sailed half the length of the field toward Nate Wright and Drew Pearson, how Pearson caught the ball off of his hip then shockingly waltzed into the end zone for a Cowboys touchdown. Nearly seven out of ten times the Vikings would have won that game in the 1970s, Staubach and the Cowboys' prayers were indeed answered that day.

# Second Quarter Answer Key

1) A – Blakeslee Stadium (It has been the home of Vikings summer training camp since 1966.)

2) D – #10 (Jersey number worn from 1961-66 and again from 1972-78.)

3) C – 2007 (RB Adrian Peterson was drafted 7th overall in the first round of the 2007 draft.)

4) A – 1970s (Minnesota left the decade of the '70s with a 99-43-2 record, for a .694 winning percentage.)

5) A – Yes (The Vikings are 51-42-2 [.548] all-time versus the Chicago Bears.)

6) C – 4 (1973 [12-2-0], 1974 [10-4-0], 1975 [12-2-0], and 1976 [11-2-1])

7) C – 72 (In Super Bowl VIII Minnesota had 72 rushing yards on 24 attempts vs. Miami [Minnesota 7, Miami 24].)

8) A – Minnesota (Bud was a three-sport letterman [football, baseball, and basketball] at the University of Minnesota from 1946-49.)

9) D – Marshall (Minnesota drafted Doug Chapman in 2000, Randy Moss in 1998, and Carl Lee in 1983.)

10) A – Yes (The Vikings are 16-4 [.800] all-time in games following a bye week.)

11) C – 49 (The St. Louis Rams scored 49 points [37-49] vs. Minnesota in the 1999 Divisional Playoff Game.)

12) A – 4 (Chicago Bears [95], Detroit Lions [95], Green Bay Packers [95], and Tampa Bay Buccaneers [51])

13) A – Yes (From 2006-08 Tarvaris has 524 total career passing attempts.)

14) D – Barry Sanders (220 yards on Nov. 24, 1991 [Minnesota 14, Detroit 34])

15) B – 56 yards (Paul Edinger kicked a 56-yard FG vs. Green Bay on Oct. 23, 2005 [Minnesota 23, Green Bay 20].)

16) C – Cris Carter (Fred Cox led the league in 1970 with 125 points and Gary Anderson in 1998 with 164 points.)

17) B – Chicago Bears (In Week 1 of the 1961 season Minnesota defeated Chicago 37-13 in their first-ever NFL regular-season game.)

18) D – Has never happened (The closest the Vikings have come to 500 yards of total offense in a postseason game was 476 at St. Louis on Jan. 16, 2000 [Minnesota 37, St. Louis 49].)

19) C – 2 (The Vikings' number-one overall picks included Tommy Mason [Tulane] in 1961 and Ron Yary [Southern Cal] in 1968.)

20) A – True (Coach Childress held various assistant coaching positions at both the college and pro levels from 1978-2005.)

21) D – 95 (Chester Taylor sprinted 95 yards for a TD at Seattle Seahawks on Oct. 22, 2006.)

22) D – None of the above (Minnesota has beaten every NFL team at home except the Baltimore Ravens, who they have yet to play there.)

23) B – Max Winter (Opened in May of 1981, the Winter Park facility is located in Eden Prairie, Minn.)

24) D – 11 (2008, 2004, 1999, 1997, 1996, 1994, 1993, 1992, 1988, 1987, and 1982)

25) A – True (SB IV [Minn. 239 total yards, Kansas City 273 total yards], SB VIII [Minn. 238, Miami 259], SB IX [Minn. 119, Pittsburgh 333], and SB XI [Minn. 353, Oakland 429])

26) D – 1969 (The Vikings earned their first-ever playoff victory vs. Los Angeles Rams on Dec. 27, 1969 [Minnesota 13, Los Angeles 2].)

27) C – 7 (Minnesota lost season openers at home in 1967, 1972, 1977, 1984, 1986, 2001, and 2005. All-time they are 17-7 [.708] in season openers at home.)

28) A – 4 (Chuck Foreman 1973, Sammy White 1976, Randy Moss 1998, and Adrian Peterson 2007)

29) D – 3 (Mike Tice played three seasons, 1992-95, for Minnesota prior to returning to coach the team from 2001-05.)

30) B – 19 (5 preseason [0-5] and 14 regular season [3-11])

31) D – 84 yards (Harry Newsome kicked an 84-yarder on Dec. 20, 1992 at Pittsburgh Steelers [Minnesota 10, Pittsburgh 5].)

32) B – No (Minnesota is 78-80-1 [.494] all-time versus current AFC teams.)

33) A – Randy Moss (Moss had 111 receptions for 1,632 yards in 2003.)

34) D – None of the above (No Viking has ever recorded 250 or more receiving yards in a single game.)

35) B – Dallas Cowboys (Dallas defeated Minnesota 28-0 in Week 4 of the 1961 season.)

36) A – Tampa Bay Buccaneers (The first regular-season game in the Metrodome took place on Sept. 12, 1982 [Vikings 17, Tampa Bay 10].)

37) D – 99 (In the third quarter of Week 13's game vs. Chicago, the Vikings scored on a 99-yard pass play from Gus Frerotte to Bernard Berrian. This was only the 11th 99-yard pass reception in NFL history [Nov. 30, 2008].)

38) B – Randall McDaniel (OG, 11 selections from 1989-99)

39) C – Daunte Culpepper (379 completions for 4,717 yards in 2004)

40) A – True (2,634 yards rushing offense and 1,185 yards rushing defense)

41) B – Sammy White (Sammy had 210 yards receiving vs. Detroit on Nov. 7, 1976 [Minnesota 31, Detroit 23].)

42) B – 2 (Joe Kapp 1967-69 and Gary Cuozzo 1970-71)

43) D – Greg Coleman (Greg punted 565 times from 1979-87 with no punts blocked.)

44) B – 3 (Scott Studwell [1,928 from 1977-90], Matt Blair [1,404 from 1974-85], and Jeff Siemon [1,375 from 1972-82])

45) A – Yes (Fran reached a total of 33,098 career passing yards for the Vikings from 1961-66 and 1972-78.)

46) D – Carl Eller (130 career sacks from 1964-78)

47) A – 2 (Randy Moss [1,632 in 2003 and 1,347 in 2002] and Cris Carter [1,274 in 2000, 1,371 in 1995, and 1,256 in 1994])

48) B – 2 (Bud Grant [1969 AP, *The Sporting News*, and *Pro Football Weekly*] and Dennis Green [1998 Maxwell])

49) B – 2 (1970s 99-43-2 [.694] and 1990s 95-65-0 [.594])

50) A – Cris Carter (Given annually by the NFL, the award recognizes a player's charity and volunteer work as well as their on-field excellence. Cris won the prestigious award in 1999.)

Note: All answers valid as of the end of the 2008 season, unless otherwise indicated in the question itself.

# *Third Quarter*    *3-Point Questions*

1) How many times has Minnesota lost in the NFC Championship game?

     A)   2
     B)   3
     C)   4
     D)   5

2) What is the Vikings' all-time record on Thanksgiving Day?

     A)   4-2
     B)   5-1
     C)   6-0
     D)   Have never played on Thanksgiving Day

3) Which year was Minnesota's first-ever 10-win season?

     A)   1969
     B)   1970
     C)   1972
     D)   1973

4) Which Vikings head coach has the second most wins while at Minnesota?

     A)   Norm Van Brocklin
     B)   Mike Tice
     C)   Jerry Burns
     D)   Dennis Green

## VIKINGOLOGY TRIVIA CHALLENGE

5) What is Minnesota's largest margin of victory in a postseason game?

    A) 30 points
    B) 32 points
    C) 34 points
    D) 39 points

6) Who holds the Vikings' career record for receiving yards?

    A) Cris Carter
    B) Anthony Carter
    C) Sammy White
    D) Randy Moss

7) Which of the following Minnesota quarterbacks never threw five touchdown passes in a single game?

    A) Tommy Kramer
    B) Daunte Culpepper
    C) Joe Kapp
    D) Fran Tarkenton

8) How many combined kickoffs and punts were returned for touchdowns by the Vikings in 2008?

    A) 0
    B) 1
    C) 2
    D) 3

## MINNESOTA VIKINGS FOOTBALL

9) What is the Minnesota record for PATs made in a single game?

    A)  5
    B)  6
    C)  7
    D)  8

10) What is the only decade the Vikings failed to have a 10-win season?

    A)  1970s
    B)  1980s
    C)  1990s
    D)  None of the above

11) Ron Yary played in the most postseason games as a Viking.

    A)  True
    B)  False

12) How many career 300-yard passing games did Viking QBs Tommy Kramer and Daunte Culpepper have?

    A)  18
    B)  19
    C)  23
    D)  24

# *Third Quarter*     *3-Point Questions*

13) How many times has a rookie led the Vikings in sacks?

     A) 1
     B) 2
     C) 3
     D) 4

14) Who is the only Vikings defender to record ten interceptions in a single season?

     A) Cory Chavous
     B) Issiac Holt
     C) Paul Krause
     D) Rip Hawkins

15) Which Vikings coach has the best career winning percentage?

     A) Dennis Green
     B) Bud Grant
     C) Brad Childress
     D) Jerry Burns

16) How many Minnesota quarterbacks have started 50 or more games?

     A) 1
     B) 2
     C) 3
     D) 4

# *Third Quarter*   *3-Point Questions*

17) Who was the most recent Viking to record greater than 150 total defensive tackles in a single season?

    A)  E.J. Henderson
    B)  Ed McDaniel
    C)  Jack Del Rio
    D)  Scott Studwell

18) What is the Vikings' record for most consecutive losses?

    A)  5
    B)  6
    C)  8
    D)  10

19) When was the last time the season-leading passer for Minnesota had fewer than 1,000 yards passing?

    A)  1963
    B)  1971
    C)  1986
    D)  Has never happened

20) Who was the last receiver to lead the Vikings in scoring?

    A)  White Sammy
    B)  Cris Carter
    C)  Randy Moss
    D)  A receiver has never led the team in scoring

21) What is Minnesota's all-time winning percentage at home (regular season and postseason)?

    A) .465
    B) .471
    C) .539
    D) .592

22) Did the Vikings ever not have official team cheerleaders?

    A) Yes
    B) No

23) Who was the most recent Viking to have his jersey number retired?

    A) Korey Stringer
    B) Mick Tingelhoff
    C) Jim Marshall
    D) Cris Carter

24) How many seasons have the Vikings gained greater than 2,500 rushing yards as a team?

    A) 0
    B) 1
    C) 2
    D) 3

# *Third Quarter*

*3-Point Questions*

25) Viking Gary Zimmerman was named to the Hall of Fame's Team of the Decade for the 1980s and 1990s.

    A)  True
    B)  False

26) How many overtime games did Minnesota play in 2007?

    A)  0
    B)  1
    C)  2
    D)  3

27) Who is the only Minnesota running back to be named NFC Rookie of the Year?

    A)  Terry Allen
    B)  Robert Smith
    C)  Adrian Peterson
    D)  Chuck Foreman

28) All-time, how many non-kickers led the Vikings in scoring?

    A)  5
    B)  7
    C)  8
    D)  10

29) Which year did Minnesota get its 500$^{th}$ all-time regular-season win?

    A) 1993
    B) 1998
    C) 2001
    D) None of the above

30) Who was the last Viking to be inducted into the Vikings Ring of Honor?

    A) John Randle
    B) Chuck Foreman
    C) Cris Carter
    D) Randall McDaniel

31) How many regular-season games did a Vikings running back rush for greater than 100 yards in 2008?

    A) 8
    B) 10
    C) 12
    D) 14

32) What is Minnesota's longest drought between playoff appearances?

    A) 2 years
    B) 3 years
    C) 4 years
    D) 5 years

33) Against which two AFC teams does Minnesota have the best all-time winning percentage (min. 3 games)?

   A)   Buffalo Bills and Oakland Raiders
   B)   Cleveland Browns and Jacksonville Jaguars
   C)   Tennessee Titans and San Diego Chargers
   D)   Denver Broncos and Pittsburgh Steelers

34) How did Minnesota score its first points in Super Bowl IV?

   A)   Rushing
   B)   Passing
   C)   Kickoff Return
   D)   Fumble Return

35) Has Minnesota ever failed to rush for 1,000 yards as a team in a season?

   A)   Yes
   B)   No

36) How many consecutive Vikings games did Jim Marshall start?

   A)   230
   B)   250
   C)   270
   D)   290

**VIKINGOLOGY TRIVIA CHALLENGE**

37) Who was the Vikings' first round pick in the 2009 NFL Draft?

    A) Asher Allen
    B) Percy Harvin
    C) Phil Loadholt
    D) Jasper Brinkley

38) Who is the only Viking to lead the team in passing and rushing in the same year?

    A) Tommy Kramer
    B) Joe Capp
    C) Randall Cunningham
    D) None of the above

39) How many Vikings Ring of Honor inductees are there?

    A) 14
    B) 15
    C) 17
    D) 20

40) When was the last season the leading rusher for Minnesota gained fewer than 500 yards?

    A) 1993
    B) 1996
    C) 1997
    D) 2000

**MINNESOTA VIKINGS FOOTBALL**

# *Third Quarter*

*3-Point Questions*

**VIKINGOLOGY TRIVIA CHALLENGE**

**41)** When was the last time the Vikings went undefeated in the preseason?

- A) 1999
- B) 2001
- C) 2003
- D) 2005

**42)** What is Minnesota's all-time record for largest margin of victory?

- A) 43 points
- B) 45 points
- C) 46 points
- D) 48 points

**43)** In which state did the Vikings hold summer practice prior to locating camp in Mankato, Minn.?

- A) Minnesota
- B) North Dakota
- C) Iowa
- D) Wisconsin

**44)** Who coached Minnesota immediately after Les Steckel?

- A) Jerry Burns
- B) Bud Grant
- C) Dennis Green
- D) Mike Tice

**MINNESOTA VIKINGS FOOTBALL**

# Third Quarter

## VIKINGOLOGY TRIVIA CHALLENGE

45) Who scored the first TD for the Vikings in the 2008 NFC Wild Card Playoff game versus the Eagles?

    A)  Bernard Berrian
    B)  Tarvaris Jackson
    C)  Adrian Peterson
    D)  Chester Taylor

46) Did Bud Grant win his final game as a Vikings head coach?

    A)  Yes
    B)  No

47) How many interceptions did the Vikings return for touchdowns in 2007?

    A)  2
    B)  4
    C)  5
    D)  6

48) How many Minnesota receivers had 50 or more receptions in the 2008 regular season?

    A)  0
    B)  1
    C)  2
    D)  3

# *Third Quarter*

49) When was the last season Minnesota led the NFL in rushing defense?

    A)  2006
    B)  2007
    C)  2008
    D)  None of the above

50) What is Minnesota's record for most consecutive playoff losses?

    A)  5
    B)  6
    C)  8
    D)  9

# *Third Quarter Viking Cool Fact*

Max Winter had a great name for a person living in Minnesota. He also had a great name in mind for a professional sports team. In 1947 he became general manager and part owner of a recently transitioned NBA franchise that would become known as the Minneapolis Lakers, despite Winter's passionate lobbying to name the team the Minnesota Vikings. Legend has it he was so sure of his success that he even bought Minnesota Vikings letterhead for his office. To his chagrin, a name-the-team contest held by a local sports radio personality and the team's front office would resolve the naming issue. Thankfully Max did not give up, he kept his dream alive and eventually when he and his partners received approval for their NFL expansion franchise he triumphantly resurrected the Minnesota Vikings name, and perhaps even made good use of some fine stationary.

# Third Quarter Answer Key

1) C – 4 (1977 [6-23 at Dallas Cowboys], 1987 [10-17 at Washington Redskins], 1998 [27-41 vs. Atlanta Falcons], and 2000 [0-34 at NY Giants])

2) B – 5-1 (All games have been played at either Dallas or Detroit. Their only loss was in 1995 at Detroit.)

3) A – 1969 (The Vikings were 12-2-0 in Bud Grant's third season has head coach.)

4) D – Dennis Green (Coach Green ended his coaching career at Minnesota with a 97-62-0 record.)

5) C – 34 points (On Jan. 3, 1988 the Vikings handed the Saints a 44-10 loss at New Orleans in the NFC Wild Card game.)

6) A – Cris Carter (12,383 receiving yards from 1990-2001)

7) D – Fran Tarkenton (Fran had 4 TDs in a single game, but never 5.)

8) B – 1 (Bernard Berrian returned a punt 82 yards for a TD at Arizona in Week 15 [Minnesota 35, Arizona 14].)

9) C – 7 (Fred Cox [vs. Baltimore and vs. Pittsburgh 1969] and Chuck Nelson [at Tampa Bay 1988])

10) D – None of the above (There was only one ten-win season in the 1960s.)

11) A – True (Yary participated in 20 career playoff games from 1968-81.)

12) B – 19 (Culpepper won 11 of his 19 career 300 yard games compared to Kramer's 9 wins.)

13) D – 4 (Alan Page 1967 [8.5], Doug Martin 1980 [5.0], Keith Millard 1985 [11.0], and Kevin Williams 2003 [10.5])

14) C – Paul Krause (Paul had 10 INTs in the 1975 regular season.)

15) B – Bud Grant (Coach Grant had a .620 [158-96-5] career winning percentage.)

16) C – 3 (Fran Tarkenton [171], Tommy Kramer [110], and Daunte Culpepper [80])

17) A – E.J. Henderson (Henderson was credited with 155 total tackles in 2007.)

18) C – 8 (The last four games of 2001 and first four games of 2002)

19) B – 1971 (Gary Cuozzo completed 75 of 168 attempts for 842 yards.)

20) C – Randy Moss (Moss tied Aaron Elling with 102 points in 2003.)

21) D – .592 (On a combined basis the Vikings own a 240-165-4 all-time regular-season and postseason record at Metropolitan Stadium and the H.H.H. Metrodome.)

22) A – Yes (The St. Louis Parkettes cheered on the Vikings prior to the team fielding its official cheerleading squad in 1984.)

23) D – Cris Carter (Chris's jersey number was retired on Sept. 14, 2003.)

24) C – 2 (2,634 rushing yards in 2007 and 2,507 in 2002)

25) A – True (The Pro Football Hall of Fame named Gary to both the 1980s and 1990s All-Decade Teams.)

26) C – 2 (Week 2 [Minnesota 17, Detroit 20 (OT)] and Week 17 [Minnesota 19, Denver 22 (OT)])

27) D – Chuck Foreman (Chuck was named UPI NFC Rookie of The Year in 1973.)

28) B – 7 (Jerry Reichow 1961 [66 points]; Chuck Forman 1974 [90 points], 1975 [132 points], & 1977 [54 points]; Sammy White 1977 [54 points]; Cris Carter 1997 [84 points]; and Randy Moss 2003 [102 points])

29) D – None of the above (The Vikings have 395 all-time victories through the 2008 season.)

30) A – John Randle (A Viking defensive tackle from 1990-2000, Randle became a Vikings Ring of Honor member on Nov. 30, 2008.)

31) B – 10 (Each 100+ yard rushing performance was put in by Adrian Peterson.)

32) D – 5 years (Five years elapsed from Minnesota's 1982 playoff appearance to their 1987 appearance.)

33) B – Cleveland Browns and Jacksonville Jaguars (The Vikings are 9-3 [.750] all-time in the Minnesota-Cleveland series. They are 3-1 [.750] all-time versus Jacksonville.)

34) A – Rushing (Dave Osborn scored on a 4-yard rushing play [Minnesota 7, Kansas City Chiefs 23].)

35) A – Yes (In 1982's strike-shortened season Minnesota had just 912 total yards rushing.)

36) C – 270 (Jim's consecutive starts streak was from 1961-79.)

37) B – Percy Harvin (Harvin was selected with the 22nd overall pick in the 2009 draft.)

38) D – None of the above (Since 1961 no Viking has led the team in both categories in the same season.)

39) C – 17 (Fran Tarkenton, Alan Page, Jim Finks, Bud Grant, Paul Krause, Fred Zamberletti, Jim Marshall, Ron Yary, Korey Stringer, Mick Tingelhoff, Carl Eller, Cris Carter, Bill Brown, Jerry Burns, Randall McDaniel, Chuck Foreman, and John Randle)

40) A – 1993 (Scottie Graham had 488 yards on 118 attempts in 1993 to lead all Vikings rushers.)

41) B – 2001 (Minnesota defeated New Orleans 28-21, Pittsburgh 24-10, Indianapolis 28-21, and Miami 20-7 to go 4-1 in 2001's preseason.)

42) D – 48 points (On Nov. 9, 1969 Minnesota defeated Cleveland 51-3 at The Met.)

43) A – Minnesota (Training camp was held in Bemidji, Minn. from 1961-65.)

44) B – Bud Grant (Coach Grant led the Vikings both immediately prior to and after Coach Steckel, who coached in 1984.)

45) C – Adrian Peterson (Peterson scored on a 40-yard run up the center of the field on the first drive of the second quarter.)

46) B – No (Coach Grant's final game was a 35-37 loss vs. Philadelphia on Dec. 22, 1985.)

47) D – 6 (This marked the second season in Vikings history that they returned 6 INTs for touchdowns. The first was in 1992.)

48) B – 1 (Bobby Wade had 53 receptions to lead all Vikings receivers in 2008.)

49) C – 2008 (Minnesota led the NFL with 76.9 yards per game. This was the second season in a row the team led the league in rushing defense.)

50) A – 5 (1989, 1992, 1993, 1994, and 1996)

Note: All answers valid as of the end of the 2008 season, unless otherwise indicated in the question itself.

# Fourth Quarter

*4-Point Questions*

1) When was the most recent season a Vikings game resulted in a tie?

    A) 1971
    B) 1978
    C) 1986
    D) 1995

2) Which opponent handed Minnesota its worst defeat in 2008?

    A) Tampa Bay Buccaneers
    B) Chicago Bears
    C) Philadelphia Eagles
    D) Tennessee Titans

3) How many Vikings have their jersey number retired?

    A) 4
    B) 5
    C) 6
    D) 7

4) Has a Vikings running back ever had five rushing touchdowns in a single game?

    A) Yes
    B) No

# *Fourth Quarter*  *4-Point Questions*

5) Which player holds Minnesota's record for most consecutive field goals made?

    A) Gary Anderson
    B) Jan Stenerud
    C) Rich Karlis
    D) Fred Cox

6) Who was the most recent head coach to win his first regular-season game with Minnesota?

    A) Mike Tice
    B) Dennis Green
    C) Brad Childress
    D) Jerry Burns

7) What is Minnesota's record for most consecutive years appearing in the postseason?

    A) 5
    B) 6
    C) 7
    D) 8

8) How many Minnesota head coaches are in the Pro Football Hall of Fame?

    A) 2
    B) 3
    C) 4
    D) 5

# *Fourth Quarter* *4-Point Questions*

9) Against which AFC team does Minnesota have the worst all-time winning percentage (min. 3 games)?

    A)  Indianapolis Colts
    B)  New England Patriots
    C)  Oakland Raiders
    D)  New York Jets

10) Did Bud Grant coach the CFL's Montreal Alouettes prior to coaching the Minnesota Vikings?

    A)  Yes
    B)  No

11) Which of the following Vikings players was not named a Consensus All-Pro in 1998?

    A)  Robert Smith
    B)  Randy Moss
    C)  Randall McDaniel
    D)  John Randle

12) When was the last season a Vikings defender had three interceptions in the same game?

    A)  1990
    B)  1995
    C)  2000
    D)  2005

# Fourth Quarter  *4-Point Questions*

13) In which of the following categories did the Vikings' Jared Allen lead the NFL in 2008?

    A) Safeties
    B) Tackles
    C) Forced Fumbles
    D) Passes Defensed

14) Who holds Minnesota's single-season rushing yards record?

    A) Robert Smith
    B) Adrian Peterson
    C) Chester Taylor
    D) Chuck Foreman

15) When was the last season the Vikings were shutout?

    A) 2004
    B) 2005
    C) 2006
    D) 2007

16) Daunte Culpepper passed for greater than 3,000 yards every season he played for Minnesota.

    A) True
    B) False

# *Fourth Quarter* *4-Point Questions*

17) Which Viking later became the first African-American quarterback enshrined in the Pro Football Hall of Fame?

    A) Daunte Culpepper
    B) Warren Moon
    C) Randall Cunningham
    D) None of the above

18) How many consecutive seasons did the Vikings' Cris Carter have greater than 1,000 yards receiving?

    A) 6
    B) 7
    C) 8
    D) 9

19) Who holds Minnesota's records for rushing touchdowns in a game, season, and career?

    A) Chuck Foreman
    B) Ted Brown
    C) Terry Allen
    D) D.J. Dozier

20) Which Minnesota quarterback holds the team record for highest passer rating in a single season?

    A) Randall Cunningham
    B) Fran Tarkenton
    C) Brad Johnson
    D) Daunte Culpepper

# *Fourth Quarter* *4-Point Questions*

**21)** How many total head coaches have the Vikings had in their history?

    A)  7
    B)  8
    C)  9
    D)  10

**22)** What is Minnesota's largest margin of victory over Chicago?

    A)  28 points
    B)  29 points
    C)  30 points
    D)  31 points

**23)** Which Vikings head coach has the second best winning percentage at Minnesota (min. 3 seasons)?

    A)  Mike Tice
    B)  Jerry Burns
    C)  Dennis Green
    D)  Brad Childress

**24)** Has Minnesota played every NFL team at least once?

    A)  Yes
    B)  No

# Fourth Quarter *4-Point Questions*

**25)** Which Viking won the Ed Block Courage Award in 2008?

    A) Chad Greenway
    B) Koren Robinson
    C) Kenechi Udeze
    D) Matt Birk

**26)** Minnesota has an all-time winning record against every NFC North opponent.

    A) True
    B) False

**27)** Which of the following Vikings defensive linemen was not a member of the Purple People Eaters?

    A) Alan Page
    B) Jim Marshall
    C) Don Hultz
    D) Gary Larsen

**28)** Who was the last Viking to lead the NFL in yards per kickoff return?

    A) Koren Robinson
    B) Darrin Nelson
    C) Jimmy Edwards
    D) None of the above

# Fourth Quarter *4-Point Questions*

29) Which decade did Minnesota have its worst winning percentage?

    A) 1960s
    B) 1980s
    C) 1990s
    D) 2000s

30) The Vikings were penalized for greater than 1,000 yards in 2008.

    A) True
    B) False

31) Which of the following is not a nickname commonly associated with the Vikings' Adrian Peterson?

    A) "A.D."
    B) "Lew-Lew"
    C) "Purple Jesus"
    D) "All Day"

32) Who is the only Super Bowl opponent to have a halftime lead against the Vikings?

    A) Pittsburgh Steelers
    B) Miami Dolphins
    C) Oakland Raiders
    D) Every Super Bowl Opponent

33) When was the last season the Vikings gave up a safety?

    A)   2006
    B)   2007
    C)   2008
    D)   None of the above

34) What is the worst defeat Minnesota suffered in a postseason game?

    A)   0-36
    B)   0-41
    C)   0-52
    D)   0-54

35) What is Minnesota's record for consecutive regular-season wins?

    A)   9
    B)   10
    C)   12
    D)   13

36) Since 1970, has Minnesota ever led the league in passing offense or total offense?

    A)   Yes
    B)   No

37) What color shoes do Vikings players currently wear?

A) Gold
B) White
C) Black
D) Any

38) When was the last season the Vikings allowed a two-point conversion?

A) 2005
B) 2006
C) 2007
D) 2008

39) Who holds Minnesota's record for most consecutive seasons leading the team in total sacks?

A) John Randle
B) Chris Doleman
C) Jim Marshall
D) Doug Martin

40) Did the Vikings travel to Miami, Fla. to play Oakland in Super Bowl XI?

A) Yes
B) No

# *Fourth Quarter* *4-Point Questions*

41) What is the largest crowd to ever attend a Vikings home game?

    A)  64,482
    B)  65,879
    C)  66,547
    D)  67,111

42) What season did the Vikings play in their first-ever NFL International Series game?

    A)  2005
    B)  2006
    C)  2007
    D)  None of the above

43) Which of the following Viking quarterbacks never had a 400-yard passing game?

    A)  Warren Moon
    B)  Daunte Culpepper
    C)  Wade Wilson
    D)  Fran Tarkenton

44) What was the best winning percentage of a Minnesota head coach who lasted one season or less?

    A)  .174
    B)  .178
    C)  .184
    D)  .188

# Fourth Quarter

*4-Point Questions*

**45)** Who was the most recent opponent Minnesota shut out?

- A) Houston Texans
- B) Detroit Lions
- C) Cincinnati Bengals
- D) Philadelphia Eagles

**46)** Who holds Minnesota's record for most points scored in a single season?

- A) Gary Anderson
- B) Fred Cox
- C) Fuad Reveiz
- D) Chuck Foreman

**47)** What are the most touchdown passes by Tommy Kramer against a single team in his career as a Viking?

- A) 4
- B) 5
- C) 6
- D) 7

**48)** What is Minnesota's record for most consecutive wins at home?

- A) 11
- B) 12
- C) 14
- D) 15

# *Fourth Quarter*

## VIKINGOLOGY TRIVIA CHALLENGE

49) Who holds Minnesota's career postseason rushing yards record?

    A) Joe Kapp
    B) Robert Smith
    C) Chuck Foreman
    D) Dave Osborn

50) What type of surface do the Vikings currently play on in the Metrodome?

    A) FieldTurf
    B) SuperTurf
    C) AstroTurf
    D) Indoor Natural Grass

# *Fourth Quarter Viking Cool Fact*

From 1963-77 Fred Cox led the Vikings in scoring. He also leads the team in another surprising category, inventing light-weight sponge-like toy footballs. One day Cox's friend John Mattox shared an idea he had for a kids' game requiring such a ball to play. John's original thought was that the ball needed to be heavy so the kids would not continually kick the ball out of the yard. Fred suggested using a softer, lighter foam rubber ball instead to prevent injuries. He developed a prototype and together they pitched the design to toymakers at Parker Brothers. Not so coincidentally Parker Brothers, the manufacturer of the already popular Nerf ball, was researching how to apply their NERF (Non-Expanding Recreational Foam) material to the shape of a football, but were having trouble because it was too light to throw properly. Eventually the Nerf football we all know and love was born. Fred Cox even appeared on advertisements for the product in the 1970s.

# Fourth Quarter Answer Key

1) B – 1978 (Minnesota and Green Bay played to a 10-10 tie on Nov. 26, 1978 at Lambeau Field.)

2) D – Tennessee Titans (Only thirteen points separated Tennessee and Minnesota in their Week-4 matchup [Minnesota 17, Tennessee 30].)

3) C – 6 (Fran Tarkenton's #10 retired in 1979, Alan Page's #88 retired in 1988, Jim Marshall's #70 retired in 1999, Korey Stringer's #77, Mick Tingelhoff's #53, and Cris Carter's #80 retired in 2003)

4) B – No (Many Vikings have scored three rushing TDs in a game, but none have scored more.)

5) A – Gary Anderson (In 1998 Anderson made 35 consecutive FGs to set the team record.)

6) C – Brad Childress (In 2006 Coach Childress led the Vikings to a 19-16 victory at Washington Redskins in his first regular-season game as head coach.)

7) B – 6 (Minnesota appeared in the postseason each season from 1973-78.)

8) A – 2 (Norm Van Brocklin [1961-66] class of 1971 and Bud Grant [1967-83 and 1985] class of 1994)

9) D – New York Jets (Minnesota has only won 1 of 8 games played against the Jets for a .125 winning percentage.)

10) B – No (He coached the Winnipeg Blue Bombers to a
105-53-2 [.663] record from 1957-66.)

11) A – Robert Smith (Randy Moss [AP, PFWA, and *TSN*],
Randall McDaniel [AP, PFWA, and *TSN*], and John
Randle [AP, PFWA, and *TSN*] other Viking First
Team All-Pros that season included Randall
Cunningham, Robert Griffith, and Gary Anderson.)

12) D – 2005 (On Nov. 13, 2005, Darren Sharper had three
INTs at New York Giants [Minnesota 24, New York
21].)

13) A – Safeties (Jared had 2 league-leading safeties in
2008.)

14) B – Adrian Peterson (Adrian's 1,760 yards rushing in
2008 surpassed Robert Smith's previous team
record of 1,521.)

15) D – 2007 (Green Bay scored 34 unanswered points vs.
Minnesota on Nov. 11, 2007.)

16) B – False (3,937 yards in 2000, 2,612 yards in 2001,
3,853 yards in 2002, 3,479 yards in 2003, and
4,717 yards in 2004)

17) B – Warren Moon (A Viking from 1994-96, Moon was
part of the Hall of Fame's Class of 2006.)

18) C – 8 (1,071 in 1993, 1,256 in 1994, 1,371 in 1995,
1,163 in 1996, 1,069 in 1997, 1,011 in 1998, 1,241
in 1999, and 1,274 in 2000)

19) A – Chuck Foreman (Chuck is co-holder of the career [52], season [13], and game [3] rushing TDs records at Minnesota.)

20) D – Daunte Culpepper (In 2004 Daunte had a 110.9 passer rating.)

21) A – 7 (Norm Van Brocklin 1961-66, Bud Grant 1967-83 and 1985, Les Steckel 1984, Jerry Burns 1986-91, Dennis Green 1992-2001, Mike Tice 2001-05, and Brad Childress 2006-Present)

22) D – 31 points (Bud Grant's Vikings stormed into Chicago on Oct 12, 1969 stealing a 31-0 victory.)

23) C – Dennis Green (Coach Green's 97-62-0 record produced a .610 career winning percentage at Minnesota.)

24) A – Yes (The fewest series games are two versus the Houston Texans and three versus the Baltimore Ravens.)

25) C – Kenechi Udeze (This award is given to a player from each NFL team who exemplifies and displays courage. Udeze was diagnosed with Leukemia in 2007. A bone marrow transplant from his brother is credited with helping to save his life.)

26) B – False (Chicago Bears [51-42-2, .548], Detroit Lions [63-30-2, .677], and Green Bay Packers [45-49-1, .479])

27) C – Don Hultz (Don's only season with Minnesota was 1963, just before the era of the Purple People Eaters.)

28) D – None of the above (Each of the players listed was ranked 2nd overall in a season, but no Viking has ever been the league's overall leader.)

29) A – 1960s (From 1961-69 Minnesota had a 52-67-7 overall record for a .440 winning percentage.)

30) B – False (Ninety total team penalties led to 692 penalty yards for Minnesota in 2008.)

31) B – "Lew-Lew" (Although Lewis is Peterson's middle name, Lew-Lew is not one of his known nicknames.)

32) D – Every Super Bowl Opponent (Minnesota did not score a single first-half point in all its Super Bowl appearances. Pittsburgh was up by two at half [2-0], Kansas City and Oakland by 16 [16-0], and Miami by 17 [17-0].)

33) C – 2008 (In Week 12, Minnesota punter Chris Kluwe ran out of the back of the end zone giving Jacksonville a safety in the game's fourth quarter [Minnesota 30, Jacksonville 12].)

34) B – 0-41 [The New York Giants handed the Vikings a 0-41 loss in the 2000 NFC Championship Game played on Jan. 14, 2001 at New York. It was the only time a Vikings team has been shutout in postseason play.)

35) C – 12 (Coach Grant led the Vikings to twelve straight victories from Week 2 through Week 13 of the 1969 regular season [12-2-0, .857].)

36) A – Yes (In 2003 Minnesota led the NFL with 6,294 yards of total offense and in 1998 they led the league with 4,328 yards of passing offense.)

37) C – Black (The Vikings discontinued the practice of wearing black shoes under Coach Steckel in 1984. They reinstituted the tradition once again in 2006.)

38) D – 2008 (Indianapolis Colt Dominic Rhodes completed a two-point conversion vs. the Vikings on Sept. 14, 2008 [Minnesota 15, Indianapolis 18].)

39) A – John Randle (From 1993-2000, eight seasons, Randle led his Viking teammates in total sacks.)

40) B – No (Super Bowl XI was played in the Rose Bowl in Pasadena, Calif. on Jan. 9, 1977.)

41) A – 64,482 (The record home crowd watched Minnesota vs. Green Bay on Nov. 2, 2003 [Minnesota 27, Green Bay 30].)

42) D – None of the above (To date Minnesota has not played in the series, which began in 2005.)

43) C – Wade Wilson (Wilson's best passing yardage performance was 391 yards [28 of 35] at home on Nov. 6, 1988 [Minnesota 44, Detroit 17].)

44) D – .188 (Les Steckel had a 3-13-0 season in 1984.)

45) B – Detroit Lions (Dec. 5, 1993, Minnesota shut out Detroit 13-0 at Detroit.)

46) A – Gary Anderson (164 points [59 PATs and 35 FGs] scored in 1998)

47) C – 6 (On Sept. 28, 1986 Kramer tallied 6 passing TDs vs. Green Bay [Minnesota 42, Green Bay 7].)

48) D – 15 (The Vikings won the first game of the streak on Dec. 1, 1974 [Minnesota 29, New Orleans 9] and its last game on Dec 5, 1976 [Minnesota 20, Green Bay 9].)

49) C – Chuck Foreman (From 1973-79 Foreman had 860 yards rushing [229 attempts, 3.8 average, and 7 TDs] in 13 postseason games played.)

50) A – FieldTurf (The stadium's playing surface has been FieldTurf since 2004. It was AstroTurf from 1987-2003 and SuperTurf from 1982-86.)

Note: All answers valid as of the end of the 2008 season, unless otherwise indicated in the question itself.

# Overtime Bonus *4-Point Questions*

1) How many career touchdown passes did Fran Tarkenton have for the Vikings?

    A)  210
    B)  219
    C)  221
    D)  239

2) What is the Vikings' longest winning streak in the Minnesota-Green Bay series?

    A)  4 games
    B)  5 games
    C)  7 games
    D)  8 games

3) How many Vikings have started in five or more Pro Bowls?

    A)  2
    B)  3
    C)  4
    D)  5

4) Minnesota has the best postseason winning percentage in the NFL.

    A)  True
    B)  False

# *Overtime Bonus* *4-Point Questions*

5) What is the name of the Vikings' current costumed mascot?

   A) Viktor the Viking
   B) Vik Tory
   C) Ragnar
   D) Vikadontis Rex

6) How many times has Minnesota played in the NFL Hall of Fame Game Series?

   A) 0
   B) 2
   C) 3
   D) 5

7) What year did the Vikings finish the season with only one win?

   A) 1962
   B) 1967
   C) 1984
   D) None of the above

8) How many Vikings have been named Pro Bowl MVP?

   A) 4
   B) 5
   C) 6
   D) 7

# *Overtime Bonus* *4-Point Questions*

9) How many touchdown drives of 80 yards or more did the Vikings have in the 2008 regular season?

    A) 6
    B) 9
    C) 10
    D) 11

10) What are the most points ever scored by Minnesota in a single game?

    A) 52
    B) 54
    C) 56
    D) 58

# *Overtime Bonus Answer Key*

1) D – 239 (From 1961-66 and 1972-78 Tarkenton set the
Vikings' record with 239 career touchdowns.)

2) C – 7 games (From the first series game between the
teams in 1975 to their first series game of 1978)

3) D – 5 (Randall McDaniel [11], Alan Page [7], Ron Yary
[7], John Randle [6], and Chris Doleman [5])

4) B – False (.419 [18-25] ranks Minnesota 22nd all-time.)

5) A – Viktor the Viking (Although Ragnar wears Viking
attire, Viktor is the team's official costumed mascot.)

6) C – 3 (1970 [Minn. 13, New Orleans 14], 1982 [Minn. 30,
Baltimore 14], and 1997 [Minn. 28, Seattle 26])

7) D – None of the above (The fewest wins were 2 in 1962.)

8) A – 4 (Fran Tarkenton [1965], Ahmad Rashad [1979],
Randy Moss [2000], and Adrian Peterson [2008])

9) D – 11 (Nine of 16 regular-season games had drives of
80 or more yards by Minnesota in 2008.)

10) B – 54 (On Oct. 18, 1970 the Vikings defeated Dallas
54-13 at Metropolitan Stadium.)

Note: All answers valid as of the end of the 2008
season, unless otherwise indicated in the question
itself.

# Player / Team Score Sheet

**Name:**_____

| First Quarter | | | Second Quarter | | | Third Quarter | | | Fourth Quarter | | | Overtime | |
|---|---|---|---|---|---|---|---|---|---|---|---|---|---|
| 1 | | 26 | 1 | | 26 | 1 | | 26 | 1 | | 26 | 1 | |
| 2 | | 27 | 2 | | 27 | 2 | | 27 | 2 | | 27 | 2 | |
| 3 | | 28 | 3 | | 28 | 3 | | 28 | 3 | | 28 | 3 | |
| 4 | | 29 | 4 | | 29 | 4 | | 29 | 4 | | 29 | 4 | |
| 5 | | 30 | 5 | | 30 | 5 | | 30 | 5 | | 30 | 5 | |
| 6 | | 31 | 6 | | 31 | 6 | | 31 | 6 | | 31 | 6 | |
| 7 | | 32 | 7 | | 32 | 7 | | 32 | 7 | | 32 | 7 | |
| 8 | | 33 | 8 | | 33 | 8 | | 33 | 8 | | 33 | 8 | |
| 9 | | 34 | 9 | | 34 | 9 | | 34 | 9 | | 34 | 9 | |
| 10 | | 35 | 10 | | 35 | 10 | | 35 | 10 | | 35 | 10 | |
| 11 | | 36 | 11 | | 36 | 11 | | 36 | 11 | | 36 | | |
| 12 | | 37 | 12 | | 37 | 12 | | 37 | 12 | | 37 | | |
| 13 | | 38 | 13 | | 38 | 13 | | 38 | 13 | | 38 | | |
| 14 | | 39 | 14 | | 39 | 14 | | 39 | 14 | | 39 | | |
| 15 | | 40 | 15 | | 40 | 15 | | 40 | 15 | | 40 | | |
| 16 | | 41 | 16 | | 41 | 16 | | 41 | 16 | | 41 | | |
| 17 | | 42 | 17 | | 42 | 17 | | 42 | 17 | | 42 | | |
| 18 | | 43 | 18 | | 43 | 18 | | 43 | 18 | | 43 | | |
| 19 | | 44 | 19 | | 44 | 19 | | 44 | 19 | | 44 | | |
| 20 | | 45 | 20 | | 45 | 20 | | 45 | 20 | | 45 | | |
| 21 | | 46 | 21 | | 46 | 21 | | 46 | 21 | | 46 | | |
| 22 | | 47 | 22 | | 47 | 22 | | 47 | 22 | | 47 | | |
| 23 | | 48 | 23 | | 48 | 23 | | 48 | 23 | | 48 | | |
| 24 | | 49 | 24 | | 49 | 24 | | 49 | 24 | | 49 | | |
| 25 | | 50 | 25 | | 50 | 25 | | 50 | 25 | | 50 | | |

____ x 1 = ____    ____ x 2 = ____    ____ x 3 = ____    ____ x 4 = ____    ____ x 4 = ____

Multiply total number correct by point value/quarter to calculate totals for each quarter.

Add total of all quarters below.

## Total Points:_____

*Thank you for playing Vikingology Trivia Challenge.*

**Additional score sheets are available at:**
www.TriviaGameBooks.com

85

# Player / Team Score Sheet

**Name:**_____

| First Quarter | | | Second Quarter | | | Third Quarter | | | Fourth Quarter | | | Overtime | |
|---|---|---|---|---|---|---|---|---|---|---|---|---|---|
| 1 | 26 | | 1 | 26 | | 1 | 26 | | 1 | 26 | | 1 | |
| 2 | 27 | | 2 | 27 | | 2 | 27 | | 2 | 27 | | 2 | |
| 3 | 28 | | 3 | 28 | | 3 | 28 | | 3 | 28 | | 3 | |
| 4 | 29 | | 4 | 29 | | 4 | 29 | | 4 | 29 | | 4 | |
| 5 | 30 | | 5 | 30 | | 5 | 30 | | 5 | 30 | | 5 | |
| 6 | 31 | | 6 | 31 | | 6 | 31 | | 6 | 31 | | 6 | |
| 7 | 32 | | 7 | 32 | | 7 | 32 | | 7 | 32 | | 7 | |
| 8 | 33 | | 8 | 33 | | 8 | 33 | | 8 | 33 | | 8 | |
| 9 | 34 | | 9 | 34 | | 9 | 34 | | 9 | 34 | | 9 | |
| 10 | 35 | | 10 | 35 | | 10 | 35 | | 10 | 35 | | 10 | |
| 11 | 36 | | 11 | 36 | | 11 | 36 | | 11 | 36 | | | |
| 12 | 37 | | 12 | 37 | | 12 | 37 | | 12 | 37 | | | |
| 13 | 38 | | 13 | 38 | | 13 | 38 | | 13 | 38 | | | |
| 14 | 39 | | 14 | 39 | | 14 | 39 | | 14 | 39 | | | |
| 15 | 40 | | 15 | 40 | | 15 | 40 | | 15 | 40 | | | |
| 16 | 41 | | 16 | 41 | | 16 | 41 | | 16 | 41 | | | |
| 17 | 42 | | 17 | 42 | | 17 | 42 | | 17 | 42 | | | |
| 18 | 43 | | 18 | 43 | | 18 | 43 | | 18 | 43 | | | |
| 19 | 44 | | 19 | 44 | | 19 | 44 | | 19 | 44 | | | |
| 20 | 45 | | 20 | 45 | | 20 | 45 | | 20 | 45 | | | |
| 21 | 46 | | 21 | 46 | | 21 | 46 | | 21 | 46 | | | |
| 22 | 47 | | 22 | 47 | | 22 | 47 | | 22 | 47 | | | |
| 23 | 48 | | 23 | 48 | | 23 | 48 | | 23 | 48 | | | |
| 24 | 49 | | 24 | 49 | | 24 | 49 | | 24 | 49 | | | |
| 25 | 50 | | 25 | 50 | | 25 | 50 | | 25 | 50 | | | |
| ___ x 1 = ___ | | | ___ x 2 = ___ | | | ___ x 3 = ___ | | | ___ x 4 = ___ | | | ___ x 4 = ___ | |

Multiply total number correct by point value/quarter to calculate totals for each quarter.

Add total of all quarters below.

## Total Points:_____

*Thank you for playing Vikingology Trivia Challenge.*

**Additional score sheets are available at:**
www.TriviaGameBooks.com

87